Giorgio Agamben

When the House
Burns Down

FROM THE DIALECT OF THOUGHT

TRANSLATED BY KEVIN ATTELL

LONDON NEW YORK CALCUTTA

The Italian List
SERIES EDITOR: Alberto Toscano

Seagull Books, 2023

First published in Italian as *Quando la casa brucia*
by Giorgio Agamben
© Giometti & Antonello, 2020

English Translation © Kevin Attell, 2022
First published in English translation by Seagull Books, 2022

ISBN   978 1 8030 9 206 5

British Library Cataloguing-in-Publication Data
A catalogue record for this book is available from the British Library

Typeset by Seagull Books, Calcutta, India
Printed and bound in the USA by Integrated Books International

When the House
Burns Down

THE ITALIAN LIST

CONTENTS

When the House Burns Down

'There is no sense in anything I do, if the house burns down.' And yet it is exactly while the house is burning that one must carry on as always, must do everything with care and precision, perhaps even more diligently—even if no one notices. Perhaps life will disappear from Earth leaving no memory of what was done, for better or for worse. But you must carry on as before; it is too late to change, there is no more time.

'For what's going on around you / is no longer your concern.' Like the geography of a country that you must leave forever. And yet, in what way does it still matter to you? At this very moment when it is no longer your concern, when everything seems finished, all things and all places appear in their true colours, touch you more closely somehow—just as they are: splendour and poverty.

Philosophy, a dead language. 'The language of poets is always a dead language . . . oddly enough: a dead language that is used to give greater life to thought.' Perhaps not a dead language but a dialect. The fact that philosophy and poetry speak in a language that is both more and less than language is the measure of their standing, of their special vitality. To weigh and judge the world by measuring it against a dialect or a dead—yet nevertheless fresh—language where there is no need to change even a comma. Continue to speak this dialect, now that the house is burning.

Which house is burning? The country where you live, or Europe, or the whole world? Perhaps the houses, the cities have already burned down—who knows how long ago?—in a single immense blaze that we pretended not to see. Some are reduced to just bits of frame, a frescoed wall, a roof beam, names, so many names, already eaten by the flames. And yet we cover them so carefully with white plaster and false words that they seem intact. We live in houses, in cities burned to the ground, as if they were still standing; the people pretend to live there and go out into the streets masked amid the ruins as if these were the familiar neighbourhoods of times past.

And now the form and nature of the flame has changed; it has become digital, invisible and cold—but exactly for this reason closer still; it encircles and envelops us at every moment.

Civilizations—barbarisms—have gone under never to rise again, and historians are used to marking and dating caesuras and wrecks. But how does one bear witness to a world that goes to its ruin with blindfolded eyes and its face covered, a republic that collapses without lucidity or pride, in fear and abjection? The blindness is all the more desperate, for the doomed believe they can steer their own wreck, swear that everything can be kept under control technically, that there is no need for a new god or a new heaven—merely prohibitions, experts and doctors. Panic and deceit.

What would a God be to whom neither prayers nor sacrifices were offered? And what would a law be that knew neither command nor execution? And a word that neither signified nor commanded but held itself truly in the beginning—indeed, before the beginning?

A culture that feels itself to be at the end, with no life left, does what it can to govern its ruin through a permanent state of exception. The total mobilization in which Ernst Jünger saw the essential character of our time must be seen from this perspective. People must be mobilized, must at all times feel themselves to be in a condition of emergency, regulated in the minimum details by those who have the power to decide on the emergency. But while in the past mobilization had the goal of bringing people closer together, today it aims to isolate and distance them from one another.

How long has the house been burning? How long ago did it burn down? Certainly a century ago, between 1914 and 1918, something happened in Europe that threw everything that still seemed whole and alive into the flames and into madness; then, once again, thirty years later, the blaze broke out everywhere and since then has not ceased to burn, without pause, quietly, barely visible below the ashes. But perhaps the fire began long before that, when humanity's blind drive towards salvation and progress joined with the power of fire and of machines. This is all well known and need not be repeated. Rather, we must ask ourselves how we continued to live and think while everything burned, ask what remained somehow whole at the centre of the blaze or at its edges. How were we able to breathe amid the flames, what did we lose, what piece of wreckage—or what illusion—did we cling to?

And now that there are no longer flames but only numbers, figures and lies, we are certainly weaker and more alone, but with no possible compromises, lucid like never before.

If it is only in the house in flames that the fundamental architectural problem becomes visible, then you can now see the stakes of the story of the West, what it sought to grasp at all costs and why it was destined to fail.

It is as if power sought at all costs to seize hold of the bare life it has produced, and yet as much as it tries to appropriate and control it with every possible apparatus—no longer just the police but also medicine and technology—bare life cannot but slip away, since it is by definition ungraspable. Governing bare life is the madness of our time. People reduced to their pure biological existence are no longer human; the government of people and the government of things coincide.

The other house, the one in which I will never be able to live but which is my true house; the other life, the one I did not live while I believed I was living it; the other language which I spelt out syllable by syllable without ever being able to speak it—so much mine that I will never be able to have them. . . .

When thought and language are divided, we believe it possible to speak while forgetting we are speaking. Poetry and philosophy, while they say something, do not forget that they are speaking; they remember language. If we remember language, if we do not forget that we can speak, then we are freer, not confined to things and rules. Language is not a tool; it is our face, the open in which we are.

The face is the most human thing; the human has a face and not simply a muzzle or a snout because we dwell in the open, because in our faces we expose ourselves and communicate. This is why the face is the place of politics. Our impolitical time does not want to see its own face; it keeps it at a distance, masks up and covers it. There must be no more faces, only numbers and figures. Even the tyrant is faceless.

To feel oneself living: to be affected by one's own sensibility, to be delicately given over to one's own gesture yet unable to assume it or avoid it. Feeling myself living makes my life possible, even if I were closed up in a cage. And nothing is so real as this possibility.

In the coming years there will be only monks and delinquents. And yet it is not possible simply to draw oneself aside, to believe one can pull oneself out from underneath the rubble of the world that has collapsed around us. For the collapse matters to us and calls to us; we, too, are only a piece of that rubble. And we will cautiously have to learn to use it in a more just way, without being noticed.

Growing old: 'growing only in the roots, no longer in the branches.' Sinking down into the roots when there are no longer flowers or leaves. Or rather like a drunken butterfly flitting about what has been lived through. There are still branches and flowers in the past. And you can still make honey of them.

The face is in God, but bones are atheist. Outside, everything pushes us towards God; inside, the stubborn, mocking atheism of the skeleton.

The fact that the soul and body are indissolubly conjoined—this is spiritual. The spirit is not a third term between the soul and the body; it is only their helpless, wonderful coinciding. Biological life is an abstraction, and it is this abstraction that we presume to govern and take care of.

There can be no salvation for us as individuals; there is salvation because there are others. And this is not for moral reasons, not because I should act for their good. Only because I am not alone is there salvation: I can be saved only as one among many, as an other among others. Alone—and this is the special truth of solitude—I do not need salvation; indeed, I am properly unsavable. Salvation is the dimension that opens because I am not alone, because there is a plurality and a multitude. Becoming incarnate, God ceased to be unique; he became a man among many. This is why Christianity had to bind itself to history and follow its fortunes to the end—and when history dies out and decays, as today seems to be happening, Christianity, too, draws near to its end. Its unhealable contradiction is that it sought, in history and through history, a salvation beyond history, and when this ends the ground beneath its feet disappears. In truth, the Church was allied not with salvation but with the history of salvation, and since it sought salvation [*salvezza*] through history, it could not but end in health [*salute*]. And when the moment came, it did not hesitate to sacrifice salvation to health.

We must pry salvation from its historical context, find a plurality that is not historical, a plurality as a way out of history.

To exit from one place or situation without entering into other territories, to leave an identity and a name without taking on others.

We can only move backwards towards the present, while in the past we walk directly on. What we call the past is nothing but our long backwards movement towards the present. Separating us from our past is the first resource of power.

What frees us from weight is breath. In breath we no longer weigh anything; we are pushed along as if in flight beyond the force of gravity.

We must learn to judge anew but with a judgement that neither punishes nor rewards, neither absolves nor condemns. An act without goal which removes existence from all finalities, which are necessarily unjust and false. Merely an interruption, an instant balanced between time and the eternal, in which flashes up the faint image of a life without end or plans, without name or memory—and is thus saved, not in eternity but *sub specie aeternitatis*. A judgement without pre-established criteria and yet political for this very reason, because it restores life to its naturalness.

To feel and to feel oneself, sensation and auto-affection, are contemporaneous. Every sensation entails feeling oneself feel; in every sensation of oneself there is the feeling of something else—a friendship and a face.

Reality is the veil through which we perceive the possible, what we can or cannot do.

It is not easy to know how to recognize which of our childhood wishes have been fulfilled. And, above all, whether the share of fulfilled wishes standing beside what cannot be fulfilled is sufficient to convince us to go on living. We are afraid of death because the share of unfulfilled wishes has grown beyond all possible measure.

'Oxen and horses have four feet: this is what I call Heaven. Putting a halter on horses and piercing the nostrils of oxen: this is what I call human. This is why I say: do not let the human destroy the Heaven within you; do not let the intentional destroy the Heavenly.'

In the burning house, language remains. Not language but the immemorial, prehistoric, weak forces that guard and remember it, philosophy and poetry. And what do they guard, what do they remember of language? Not this or that meaningful proposition, not this or that article of faith or of bad faith. Rather, the very fact that there is language, that without name we are open in the name, and in this open, in a gesture, in a face we are unknowable and exposed.

Poetry, the word, is the only thing left to us from when we did not yet know how to speak, a dark song within language, a dialect or an idiom that we are unable to fully understand but which we cannot but listen to—even if the house is burning, even if in their burning language people continue to talk nonsense.

Is there, though, a language of philosophy, as there is a language of poetry? Like poetry, philosophy dwells entirely within language and it is only the way of this dwelling that distinguishes it from poetry. Two tensions in the field of language that cross each other at a certain point only then to tirelessly separate themselves. And whoever speaks a right word, a simple, fresh word, dwells within this tension.

Those who realize that the house is burning can be led to look with disdain and contempt upon their peers who seem not to realize it. And yet won't these people who do not see and do not think be precisely the lemurs to whom you will have to answer on the last day? Realizing that the house is burning does not raise you above the others: on the contrary, they are the ones with whom you will have to exchange a last glance when the flames draw nearer. What will you be able to say to justify your supposed conscience to these people who are so unknowing that they almost seem innocent?

In the burning house you continue to do what you had done before—but you cannot avoid seeing that the flames now show you bare. Something has changed, not in what you do but in the way in which you let it go in the world. A poem written in the burning house is truer, more right, because no one can hear it, because nothing ensures that it can escape the flames. But if, by chance, it finds a reader, then that reader will in no way be able to draw away from the apostrophe that calls out from that helpless, inexplicable, faint clamour.

Only someone who is unlikely ever to be heard can tell the truth, only someone who speaks from within a house that the flames are relentlessly consuming.

Humankind today is disappearing, like a face in the sand erased on the shore. But that which is taking its place no longer has a world; it is only a bare life, mute and without history, at the mercy of the calculations of power and science. Perhaps it is only beginning with this ruin that something else can one day slowly or suddenly appear—not, to be sure, a god, but neither another human—a new animal, perhaps, an otherwise living soul. . . .

Door and Threshold

To finally discover
that pleasure has no doors and that
if it does they're wide open, and
that we could have stayed outside
both of us ill-equipped and surrendering equally
playing at door and keys
with me as the door and you as the keys.

Patrizia Cavalli [1]

In his design for the entrance to the Istituto Universitario di Architettura di Venezia (IUAV), which had been commissioned in the 1960s by the university council and for

1 Patrizia Cavalli, 'The Keeper' (Gini Alhadeff trans.) in *My Poems Won't Change the World: Selected Poems* (Gini Alhadeff ed.) (New York: Farrar, Straus and Giroux, 2013), p. 231. All notes are by the translator.

which he was asked to use an Istrian stone door recovered during the restoration of the Convento dei Tolentini, Carlo Scarpa decided to lay the door flat on the ground and immerse it in water. And that is how those entering the ex-convent from the large eponymous square can see it—not without surprise—in the posthumous execution of the project completed twenty years later by Sergio Los. The horizontal placement of an essentially vertical structure such as a door could not have been anything but carefully considered.

The term 'door' has two different meanings that often tend to get confused in use. On the one hand it means an opening, an entrance, and on the other the panel that closes or opens it. In the first sense the door is essentially a passage or threshold; in the second it is rather the structure that closes off and separates one space from another. The entrance-door is an empty space, defined on either side by a wall, on the bottom by a threshold, and above by an architrave; the panel-door is an object constructed of any number of materials, usually attached to the wall by hinges on which it turns to open or close, allowing or impeding passage.

Since the threshold-door is almost always accompanied by a panel-door, the two realities are often confused to such a degree that Georg Simmel could define the door in contrast to a bridge precisely by the possibility of its being closed.

> With respect to the relation 'separateness–unification' the bridge emphasizes the latter, and it makes obvious the distance between its resting points, and makes it measurable. By doing so, it also overcomes this distance at the same time. The door, however, in a stricter and more obvious manner demonstrates that the acts of separating and relating are but two sides of the same act. . . . Exactly because the door can be opened, its being shut gives a feeling of being shut out that is

stronger than the feeling emanating from just a solid wall.[2]

The classical world was familiar with horizontal doors. In all likelihood one of these was the *mundus*, the circular hole that Romulus had dug out upon founding the city which put into communication the world of the living with the underworld of the dead. This would be opened three times a year, and, Festus tells us, during those days (which were thus considered *religious*), 'that which was hidden and secret in the cult of the Manes was brought to light and revealed' and all public activities were consequently suspended. The *mundus*, which ancient sources describe as a pit (*bothros*) or a very deep well (*altissimus puteus*), also included a panel-door, a stone, called *manalis lapis*, stone of the Manes, which would be lifted on the given days, when it would be said that *mundus patet*, the world is open.

---

2 Michael Kaern, 'Georg Simmel's *The Bridge and the Door*', *Qualitative Sociology* 17(4) (1994): 409.

Other sources tell us that the name *mundus* was also given to the narrow opening in Sicily through which Proserpina was taken away to Hades. The 'black door of Dis' near Lake Avernus, through which Aeneas descended into the underworld, is instead open night and day (*noctes atque dies patet atri ianua Ditis* [*Aeneid* 6.127]). This is a threshold-door which is easy to cross once (*facilis descensus Averno*), but arduous and risky to return through (*sed revocare gradum . . . hoc opus, hic labor est* [6.128]).

We are so used to thinking of the two types of door as inseparable that we forget not only that they are distinct but that in a certain sense they serve opposite functions. In the entrance-door the essential thing is the crossing of a threshold, while in the panel-door it is the possibility of closing or opening a passage. We can therefore say that the panel-door is a device invented to control threshold-doors, to limit the unconditional opening that these represent. This is also the reason for the endless ranks of guardians of the door, angels or doormen, latches and digital codes, that must ensure that the device functions correctly and permits entry to no one who does not have the right.

There are, however, even more sophisticated and implacable mechanisms to guarantee the inviolability of the threshold. One of these is the sanction that in Roman law punished with death anyone who transgressed a prohibited threshold, for example—beginning with the legendary killing of Remus—the walls of the city. As the term suggests (*sanctio*), the wall thus becomes *sanctus*, that is, in the words of Ulpian, '*ab iniuria hominum defensum atque munitum*', 'defended and protected against the offense of men'. And based on this model the jurists began to consider the law 'sacred'—the beginning of the paradigm of 'inviolability' which originally defined the regime of the threshold. The law is the panel-door that prohibits or permits the passage of actions among the thresholds that articulate the relations among men. As

Kafka's parable unequivocally shows, the law coincides with its own door; it is nothing other than a door.

Scarpa breaks entirely with this conception. The door laid flat is not a panel-door and the water that covers it implies that it can never be closed. (Moreover, Venice—of which Scarpa's door is, perhaps, something like an invocation—has no need of city gates: to enter it one has to cross a threshold which is the water of the lagoon, just as to get to the submersed door one has to set foot in the water). But neither is it a threshold-door, since the horizontal placement seems to emphasize the impossibility of crossing it. In a similar way, in the decoration of Palazzo Abatellis in Sicily, Scarpa had hung a Gothic stone doorway in mid-air on a wall where no access was possible. If the door is not a place but the passage and entranceway between two places, here it seems to become a place unto itself—perhaps the place par excellence, whose possible use is, however, not yet clear. In each case, the horizontal door now defines a space in which it would be possible to walk, pause to think, hesitate, perhaps even live—but not to close it or simply go across. The 'entrance' [*adito*] has become an 'area' [*ambito*]: the passage from one place to another, expressed by the preposition *ad*, cedes its place to the path—expressed by the particle *ambi*—that leads around a certain territory, patiently follows its outline.

One sphere in which panel-doors are common is the fable. Everyone knows the story of the young bride of Bluebeard, who was allowed to open all the doors of the palace save one, and who inserted the key in the precise door that the husband had prohibited her from opening, only to discover what she should not have and would not have wanted to see, namely, the bodies of the six wives that preceded her. In a religious variant, 'The Virgin Mary's Child', the one who violates the prohibition is the woodcutter's daughter whom the Madonna had taken with her to Paradise and who, instead of the twelve rooms which she was permitted to open, insists on entering the thirteenth, where she is dazzled by a vision of the Trinity. Whether the latch hides something marvellous (the splendour of the Trinity) or horrifying (the bodies of the wives), in each case it is something that one should not see or know. The panel-door, therefore, is the figure of transgression and guilt and, as Paul says of the commandments of the Torah, the door exists so that sin might abound.

'Rites de passage—this is the designation in folklore for the ceremonies that attach to death and birth, to marriage, puberty, and so forth. In modern life, these transitions are becoming ever more unrecognizable and impossible to experience. We have grown very poor in threshold experiences.'[3] The accuracy of Benjamin's diagnosis here does not seem to need further comment. No less important, though, is the sentence that follows a few lines down: 'The threshold [*Schwelle*] must be carefully

3 Walter Benjamin, *The Arcades Project* (Howard Eiland and Kevin McLaughlin trans) (Cambridge, MA: Belknap Press, 1999), p. 494.

distinguished from the boundary [*Grenze*]. A *Schwelle*
<threshold> is a zone. Transformation, passage, wave
action [*Wandel, Übergang, Fluten*] are in the word *schwellen*,
swell, and etymology ought not to overlook these
senses.'[4] The character of the threshold as a place (*Zone,*
which indicates a wide band-like portion of space) is force-
fully asserted here: suggesting a relation to the verb
schwellen (which etymologists reject), the threshold
becomes a space in which transformations, passages and
even phenomena of ebb and flow as in the sea can occur.
In each case, it is a space (like the 'zone' created by Scarpa)
that possesses properties that distinguish it from others
and not simply a border to cross.

The thesis according to which modernity has lost the
experience of the threshold must, in truth, be a bit more
nuanced. To be sure, rites of passage, which in traditional
societies marked the phases of life for both individuals and
the collective, are in decline everywhere. This, however,

---

4 Benjamin, *The Arcades Project,* p. 494.

does not mean that thresholds have simply been erased. Rather, we could say that in the absence of the rituals that make them visible they tend to expand beyond all measure. This is what has happened to adolescence, which, in industrialized societies, extends indefinitely to the point of coinciding with one's entire existence.

There is, furthermore, a sphere in which the experience of the threshold has not only not been forgotten but is indeed the object of particular attention. This is the sphere of art. Beginning at a certain point which coincides with the avant-gardes of the early twentieth century, artists seem to concentrate their efforts no longer on the production of works of art but on the paradoxical attempt to grasp a threshold where artistic creation can exist as such, independent of its works. Both the Dadaists and the surrealists thus sought to situate the artist in the immaterial gap that at once united and separated art and life, the work of art and the industrial product, the conscious and the unconscious. And yet, on this instable threshold they wanted to install themselves as guardians, preserving at all costs an artistic identity that no longer had any sense. Thus the entrance-door newly became a panel-door; the door to the museum, from which they thought they had exited, closed once again behind them.

In Latin there are at least four terms for door: *foris* (or *fores*) which has disappeared in the romance languages except for its survival in the adverbial forms *foris, foras*, 'outside [*fuori*]'. This meant less the door as a material object than the entrance to the *domus*, understood not as the building but as the seat of the family. This is why the adverb *foris* is opposed to *domi* and means that which is outside the familial sphere. *Porta* (like the Greek *peiro*, across) evokes, rather, the idea of a passage, while *ostium*, from which derives the Italian word 'uscio' (doorway), simply indicates an opening (*os*, mouth). Finally, *ianua* (essentially connected with Janus, the two-faced god) names a threshold that faces in both directions and, in Rome, a covered passageway where bankers and money changers would circulate. The basic idea, once again, is that of a passage, an entranceway, which only in the case of *foris* seems to acquire the meaning of a separation between what is inside (included) and what is outside (excluded). The decisive point, however, is that the idea of an 'outside [*fuori*]' is expressed with a term that literally means 'at the door' (*foris, foras*). The 'outside' is not another space cleanly separated from the inside by a border: the 'foreigner [*forestiero*]' and the 'outsider [*forastico*]' originally stand on the threshold; they experience the outsideness [*foraneità*] of the door.

It is, then, possible to think of the door as neither an entranceway that leads to another place nor simply a space around which one could walk. It is rather the event of an outside, which is nevertheless not another place but, as in Kant's definition of the thing-in-itself, a space that must remain absolutely empty, a pure exteriority. This is the pure exteriority that is perfectly expressed by the horizontal door of the IUAV: the space whose borders the eye can peruse is also an opening that does not lead to any determinable place but faces the sky and dwells in a pure taking place, showing the intimate outsideness of every door.

Commenting on the conception of the separate intellect that Aristotle develops in *De anima*, Alexander of Aphrodisias defines the intellect with the adverb *thurathen*, at the door (from the Greek *thura*, door). This implies that thought, too, is something like a door and that the thinker above all has an experience of an outside and an exteriority. For Alexander this threshold is where the individual is united with the active intellect that stands above and transcends the individual; for us, as Hannah Arendt suggests in her book on Eichmann, this is rather a zone of suspension, wherein the ceaseless discourse of our common images and words is interrupted for a moment. And in the cessation of thought in this empty and far-off zone, something like an outside, a space of freedom becomes possible.

In the Jewish tradition *maqom*, place, is one of the names of God. Taking seriously Paul's assertion that we live and move and have our being in God, a medieval heresy —which we know only through the testimony of the theologians who condemned its followers to the stake— asserted that God is nothing other than the taking place of each and every thing, both the stone and the worm, the angel and the man. What is divine is the being-worm of the worm, the being-stone of the stone, and what is just and good is that the world is thus, that something can appear and assume a face, in its finiteness and in its divine place.

We do not betray the thought of Amalric of Bena if we say that when we perceive the being in God of that worm or that stone they then appear to us like a door, but one that does not lead in any direction or to any place but opens to that place of all places that is God. Just as we can neither open nor close this door, we also cannot pass through it. And as the water of Scarpa's submersed door reflects the sky, becomes sky, so the creature-door is only outside of itself in the open, happily removed from the both the law of keys and the law of thresholds.

Lessons in the Darkness

א

Aleph

The position of the prophet is a particularly uncomfortable one today, and the few who attempt to take it on often seem to lack all legitimacy. Indeed, the prophet addresses the darkness of his time but, in order to do so, he must let it crash upon him and cannot expect—by means of some special gift or virtue—to retain his lucidity intact. To the Lord who calls him, Jeremiah responds with a stutter—'Ah, ah, ah'—and then adds, 'behold, I cannot speak, for I am a child.'

ב

Beth

To whom does the prophet speak? To a city, a people. The peculiarity of his apostrophe, however, consists in the fact that it cannot be understood, that the language in which he speaks appears obscure and incomprehensible. Indeed, the efficacy of his word is precisely a function of its remaining unheard, of its being in some way misunderstood. In this sense, what is prophetic is the infantile word that addresses someone who by definition cannot hear it. And it is precisely the necessary presence of both of these elements—the urgency of the apostrophe and its uselessness—that defines prophecy.

ג

Gimel

Why do the words of the prophet remain unheard? Not because they denounce the guilt of his peers and the darkness of his times. Rather, it is because the object of prophecy is the presence of the Kingdom, its discreet intrusion into every story and every gesture, its persistent taking place here and now, at every instant. What contemporaries are neither willing nor able to see is their daily intimacy with the Kingdom. And, at the same time, their living 'as though they were not the Kingdom'.

ד

Daleth

In what way does the Kingdom come to pass; in what way
is it present? Not as a thing, a group, a church, or a political party. The Kingdom always coincides with its
announcement; it has no other reality than the word—
the parable—that speaks it. It is now a mustard seed, now
a weed, now a net cast in the sea, a pearl—not as something that the words signify but only as the announcement they make of it. That which comes, the Kingdom,
is the word of announcement itself.

ה

He

To hear the word of the Kingdom therefore means to have an experience of the springing forth of the word, of a word that forever remains illegible and to come, that lies alone and primordial in the mind, with unknown provenance and unknown direction; it means to gain access to another experience of language, to a dialect or idiom that no longer designates by way of grammar and names, lexicon and syntax—and must pay this price so that it may announce and announce itself. This announcement, this meaningless, integral transformation of the word is the Kingdom.

ו

Waw

To have an experience of the springing forth of the word means to go back against the grain and retrace the long historical process through which we have interpreted our being speakers as a matter of having a language, one made of names and grammatical and syntactical rules that allow for meaningful discourse. That which was the result of much patient work of reflection and analysis has thus been projected into the past as a real presupposition, as if the grammar we have constructed were truly the original structure of the word. The Kingdom is nothing, in this sense, but the restitution of the word to its nature as dialect and announcement, beyond or before every language.

ז

Zayin

Whoever achieves this experience of the word, whoever is, in this sense, a poet and not solely a reader of his word, catches sight of its signature in every minimal fact, bears witness to it, without arrogance or bombast, in every event and every circumstance, as if clearly perceiving that everything that happens to him, in proportion with the announcement, sheds all extraneousness and all power, is at once most intimate and most remote to him.

ח

Heth

The obscurity of the announcement, the misunderstanding that its word produces in the one who does not understand it, turns back on the one who pronounces it, separates him from his people and from his own life. The announcement then becomes lament and execration, criticism and accusation, and the Kingdom becomes a threatening sign or a lost paradise—in any case, no longer intimate and present. His word no longer knows how to announce: it can only foretell or regret.

ט

Teth

The Kingdom is not a goal that must be reached, the coming endpoint of a worldly or heavenly economy. It is not a matter of imagining and bringing about more just institutions or less tyrannous states. Nor of envisioning a long and cruel transitional phase after which Justice will rule on earth.

The Kingdom is already here, daily and humble, and yet irreconcilable with the powers that try to disguise or hide it, try to prevent the recognition and love of its coming, or try to transform it into a future event. The word of the Kingdom does not produce new institutions or constitute law: it is the destituent potentiality that, in every sphere, deposes powers and institutions, including those—churches or political parties—that believe they are its representative and embodiment.

י

Yod

The experience of the Kingdom is therefore an experience of the potentiality of the word. Above all, what this word destitutes is the language. Indeed, it is not possible to depose the powers that today dominate the earth without first deposing the languages that ground and support them. Prophesy is the consciousness of the essentially political nature of the idiom in which it speaks. (Hence, too, the irrevocable pertinence of poetry to the sphere of politics).

 כ

Kaph

To destitute a language is the most difficult task. Indeed, a language, which in itself is merely a group of dead letters, pretends—but it is a pragmatic fiction which constitutes its most proper force—to contain within itself the living voice of humans, pretends to have its place, life and foundation in the voice of those who speak. In every respect, grammar refers back to this hidden voice, captures it in its letters and phonemes. But there is no voice in languages. And ours is the time in which languages everywhere show their emptiness and aphonia, become chatter or scientific formalism. The idiom of the Kingdom returns the voice to its taking place outside of languages.

ל

Lamed

The field of *language itself* [*linguaggio*] is the place of a
ceaseless conflict between the word and a given language,
between idiom and grammar. We must free ourselves
from the prejudice which holds that the word is a putting
to work, a diligent application of a given language, as if
that language already existed somewhere as a substantial
reality and as if every time we spoke we had to open a
grammar book or consult a dictionary. It is clear that languages exist only in use. What, then, is this use if it is not
a faithful and obedient execution of a language but on the
contrary an unravelling of it—or rather of its guardians,
both within and outside of us, who ensure that what we
say to each other is always traced back to the form and
identity of a language?

מ

Mem

In Dante the conflict is that between the vernacular and
the grammatical language, and between the municipal
vernaculars and the illustrious vernacular. It is a contrast
both ambiguous and risky, tireless and compliant, in the
course of which the idiom is always in the process of
falling back into a language, just as the vernacular in time
became—against the intentions of the poet—the Italian
language. Because of this, dialects today have taken the
place of the vernacular for us; they are once again a word
that 'comes from that place where it is neither writing nor
grammar'.

ב

Nun

We give the name 'dialect'—in any language—to the bringing forth of the word. And 'thought' to the illustrious vernacular that poetically draws dialect not towards another grammar but towards a language that is absent and yet, like a perfumed panther, is attested and announced in every idiom and speech.

ס

Samekh

What do we do when we speak if this is not a matter of putting the lexicon and grammar of a language to work, of articulating the voice in names and propositions? When we speak we enter into the open; we let things appear in their being both manifest and concealed: sayable but never said, present but never as objects. And yet, we forget immediately; the things of which we speak hide from us the fact that we are speaking of them, become objects of discourse and communication, and depart from the open and the Kingdom.

This falling into meaningful discourse is not, however, separated in some other place: everything happens within language, within our speaking, which is both the speech of the Kingdom and the objectifying language, dialect and grammar. And the coming and going from one to the other, both in flight and harmony, in divergent accord, is poetry.

ע

Ayin

Names do not say things: they call them into the open; they keep them in their appearing. Propositions do not carry a message: the snow-being-white [*l'esser-la-neve-bianca*] is not the content of the proposition 'the snow is white', which we never pronounce in this neutral way. The snow-being-white is its sudden, joyous, immaculate appearing to our sight on a winter morning. It is an event, not a fact.

In names and propositions we go beyond names and propositions, all the way to the point where things appear to us for an instant without name in their having a name, untasted in their being said, like a god that is felt and unknown.

Testimony and Truth

No one / bears witness for the / witness
Paul Celan

I

The truth of testimony has nothing to do with its semantic content; its truth does not depend on what it says. To
be sure, testimony can take the form of a proposition but,
in contrast to what happens in legal testimony, what it
says cannot be submitted to verification—it cannot be
true or false. Testimony is not an apophantic *logos* in
the Aristotelian sense, a discourse that says something
about something. Neither is it a prayer, an invocation or
a command. In so far as it is not defined on the basis of

what it says, testimony is always true: it simply either is or is not.

The truth of testimony does not depend on what it says but on what is not said, on the fact that it brings a speechlessness into words. The witness is someone who uniquely speaks in the name of an inability to speak. And this does not simply mean that the witness speaks for someone who cannot—for the dead, for animals, for the stones, for the grass, for the insane. The silence to which his words bear witness is internal to testimony itself; the one who bears witness to the truth is the first to fall silent before it. The witness's testimony is true to the extent that he experiences the impossibility of stating the truth in a proposition. The truth cannot have the form of a true proposition: truth can only be testified to.

This means that the witness is not the subject of knowledge. The truth that testimony entails can never present itself as such to intentional consciousness, whose knowing is necessarily articulated in the form of a discourse that says something about something. Testimony begins when the subject of knowledge is left speechless. The experience that seals the lips of the subject opens those of the witness. This does not mean that the subject is simply set aside, that it has nothing to do with the witness. It is exactly the subject's being rendered speechless that constitutes the possibility of testimony. The witness bears witness for—in the place of—the subject. The subject of knowledge does not precede testimony; it comes about, so to speak, *a posteriori* through testimony.

In the beginning there is only silence, *Sigē*. The witness transforms silence into a speechlessness and can do so only by attesting to a subject that cannot speak the truth. The silence of the subject opens the space of testimony. There are two lines: *Sigē*-testimony-truth and *Logos*-subject-knowledge, which run along one single plane and cross each other at every point. Witness and subject are the two faces of a single testimony, like the witness and the 'Muslim' at Auschwitz.

II

Aristotle seems not to give much consideration to testimony. He discusses in the *Rhetoric*, listing it among the empirical types of evidence alongside laws, contracts, tortures and oaths. He writes:

> As to witnesses [*marturoi*], there are two kinds, the ancient and the recent; and these latter, again, either do or do not share in the risks of the trial. By 'ancient' witnesses I mean the poets and all other notable [*gnorimoi*, well-known] persons whose judgments are known to all. Thus the Athenians appealed to Homer as a witness about Salamis; and the men of Tenedos not long ago appealed to Periander of Corinth in their dispute with the people of Sigeum (1375b: 26–31).[1]

---

1 Aristotle, *Rhetoric* (W. Rhys Roberts trans.) in *The Complete Works of Aristotle*, VOL. 2 (Jonathan Barnes ed.) (Princeton, NJ: Princeton University Press, 1984), p. 2191. All subsequent quotations are from the same edition.

Among the ancient witnesses that the orators evoke in their discourses, Aristotle also cites proverbs. More than veritable evidence, what these represent is the authority of tradition, which is forced to bear witness in favour of presumably deficient argumentation.

The case of recent witnesses is different. Among these Aristotle considers 'well-known people who have expressed their opinions about some disputed matter' if these opinion are useful support for the claim at hand and, finally, 'those witnesses who share the risk of punishment if their evidence is pronounced false', that is, witnesses in the proper sense, who can testify only that 'an action was or was not done, that something is or is not the case,' but not 'to the quality of an action, to its being just or unjust, useful or harmful' (1376a: 8–15). In general, 'most trustworthy of all are the ancient witnesses, since they cannot be corrupted' (1376a: 17).

It is obvious that the link between these well-known witnesses and the truth is extremely labile and contingent.

And it is a similar, purely trial-like testimony to which Kierkegaard contrasts his idea of a 'witness to the truth', who is exactly the opposite of a well-known person. 'A witness to the truth, one of the genuine witnesses to the truth, is a man who is scourged, maltreated, dragged from one prison to another, and then at last . . . crucified, or beheaded, or burnt, or roasted on a gridiron, his lifeless body thrown by the executioner in an out-of-the-way place'.[2] Here, too, testimony has nothing to do with the semantic content of a message; indeed, the special authority that it conveys to such a witness 'becomes qualitatively apparent when the content of the message or of the action is posited as indifferent'.[3] The witness to the truth cannot provide evidence for what he claims, just as it

2 Søren Kierkegaard, *Kierkegaard's Attack Upon 'Christendom,' 1854–1855* (Walter Lowrie ed.) (Princeton, NJ: Princeton University Press, 1944), p. 7.

3 Søren Kierkegaard, 'Of the Difference between a Genius and an Apostle' in *The Present Age and Of the Difference between a Genius and an Apostle* (Alexander Dru trans.) (New York: Harper and Row, 1962), p. 96.

would be absurd to 'require a *physical* certainty that God exists'.[4] His testimony shows the truth of what he affirms only on the condition that it is resolutely removed from the plane of facts and verifiable propositions.

III

What is the truth to which the witness bears witness? It is not the datum in its non-linguistic factuality, which in itself is obscure and impenetrable, nor is it the name that merely signifies it, which in itself is equally closed to that which it names. And yet, precisely towards these two uncommunicating abstractions are directed the discourses and opinions of speaking people, who forget what is at issue in their being speakers. Speakers are thus divided into ideologues, who stubbornly seek out facts and consider their being in language purely accessory and, as they say, superstructural, and communicators, for whom the

---

4 Kierkegaard, 'Of the Difference between a Genius', p. 95.

information—the medium—is entirely substituted for the thing.

The truth to which the witness bears witness is instead the thing in its being named by the name and the name insofar as it names the thing—that is, the thing in its unconcealedness, or, in the words of the poet, the being 'knowable in the medium of its appearance'.[5] It is precisely this truth, this pure knowability, that cannot be thematized as such in a proposition but only shown as a caesura or interruption in it.

What the linguistic medium cannot say, what the witness cannot speak of, is mediality itself, language as such. Knowledge can be spoken of, but of the knowability that renders knowledge possible there is nothing to say. This is the silence that the witness brings to words.

---

5 Friedrich Hölderlin, 'Anmerkungen zum Oedipus' in *Sämtliche Werke*, VOL. 5 (Friedrich Beissner ed.) (Stuttgart: W. Kohlhammer, 1952), p. 195.

IV

To whom is testimony addressed? Certainly not to contemporaries, who by definition cannot hear it. But neither is it addressed to the future generations. Indeed, the witness is placed somehow always in the last days and speaks to a world that to his eyes is ending or already ended, and someone who bears witness to the end clearly cannot count on a coming generation. The truth of testimony never stands at the beginning; it is always constitutively at the end—it is, in every sense, a final or penultimate truth.

If the witness were to address someone, present or future, this person could in turn bear witness for him, confirm his testimony, recognize its truth. But a testimony that needs an ulterior testimony loses its value and is no longer a testimony of the truth. This is why the poet has made clear that 'no one / bears witness for the / witness', that he is always alone in his testimony. Does this mean that testimony is useless and futile, that it speaks to no one and stands, so to speak, outside of history and time? Does it mean that the witness addresses his word to God, to animals, to the grass, to the stones—but not to humans? That no one can therefore bear witness for him? Or, rather, no one bears witness for the witness because the time for which the witness bears witness is the past and the people whom he addresses are dead and the dead cannot bear witness. But as soon as the witness addresses the past it is no longer the past; it can no longer pass and is as if driven helpless and wordless into the heart of the present.

What does it mean to bear witness for the dead? Isn't this what every witness does, especially if the witness is a *superstes*, a survivor? Anyone who is a survivor necessarily has to do with the dead, not to mention a dead one within himself. But in this sense is not everyone a survivor; might this not be what defines the human being against the other living beings, that we constitutively have to do with the past and with the dead? And not only because from the very beginning humans have performed funeral rites and practices that in various ways maintain relations with those who have lived before—in a deeper and more essential sense humans are made of the past and live every day conjuring and remembering that which is no longer and yet still burns inside us. We are the living being that has a past and must at every moment contend with it, bear witness for it.

Since it is addressed to the past, to its own past, testimony is essentially faithful; it has the very form of faithfulness. This does not simply mean that it must be truthful, that the witness must be sincere. Faithfulness is the intimate and unreserved adhesion to that of which, and for which, one bears witness. 'For which' here means 'in the place of'. To bear witness in the place of someone who cannot bear witness entails putting oneself in his place, assuming his name, body and voice: it entails, in this sense, being faithful to him, faithful to the point of abolishing oneself and disappearing in him. There are no living witnesses; to bear witness means above all to die.

This is why the witness cannot lie—false testimony is not a testimony.

The witness bears witness for the dead and for the past in place of the dead. But not for the dead and for the past insofar as they spoke and speak—to remember the word of the past is rather the task of memory. The witness bears witness for the silence of the dead and of the past, and this silence is more difficult to bear, more painful to remember than their word. We happily sustain what we say and the stories we tell with the words of the dead— of their silence we can only bear witness.

V

During the dialogue with Pilate in the praetorium, after having affirmed that his kingdom is not of this world, Jesus answers the question, 'So you are a king?' with these words: 'You say that I am a king. For this I was born, and for this I came into the world, to testify to the truth (*hina*

martureso tei aletheia' (John 18:37). The famous reply of
the prefect of Judea, 'What is the truth?' is not so much a
philosophical objection the idea of one truth as it is rather
a question that is perfectly appropriate in a trial when fac-
ing a defendant who stubbornly will not answer in an
unequivocal way. Jesus was supposed to answer whether
or not he was the king of the Jews; instead he unexpect-
edly ties truth and testimony into a knot and claims to be
bearing witness for the truth, as if testimony had nothing
to do with the object of a trial (whether he is or is not a
king) but entailed his entire existence ('For this I was born,
and for this I came into the world').

The issue at hand in such a testimony had been stated
by Jesus in the course of another trial, when the Pharisees
brought him before the adulteress, who according to
Mosaic law should be stoned, and asked him to pronounce
a judgement ('Now what do you say?'). Here too, instead
of answering, Jesus kneels down and writes on the ground
with his finger. Faced with their arrogant insistence he
does not issue a verdict but introduces a condition: 'Let

anyone among you who is without sin be the first to throw a stone at her' (8:7). And after taking leave of the woman he brusquely makes a claim about himself—'I am the light of the world. Whoever follows me will never walk in the darkness'—which the Pharisees, as Pilate would later do, take, not without reason, as a testimony inadmissible in a trial: 'You are testifying on your own behalf (*peri seautou martureis*); your testimony is not true (*hē marturia sou ouk estin alēthēs*).' Not only is a testimony about oneself obviously not a testimony but in this case it is doubly inappropriate since it is given in place of a judgement that had been explicitly requested.

The laconic doctrine of testimony that Jesus develops at this point must be carefully considered. Jesus begins by affirming the validity of his testimony ('Even if I testify on my own behalf, my testimony is true') and then immediately declares it to be equivalent to a judgement. Indeed, not only are self-testimony and judgement placed on the same level but the former takes the place of the latter, because testimony is not one single thing but two things in one: 'You judge according to the flesh; I judge no one. Yet even if I do judge, my judgement is true (*hē krisis hē emē alēthinē estin*); for it is not I alone who judge, but I and the Father who sent me. In your law it is written that the testimony of two witnesses is true. I testify on my own behalf (*ho marturōn peri emautou*), and the Father who sent me testifies on my behalf' (8:16–8).

The witness is split in two: the first, bearing witness on his own behalf, pronounces a testimony that is inadmissible but becomes true because it contains another that guarantees its legitimacy and substitutes it for judgement. In this case, too, the second witness bears witness for one who cannot bear witness and brings to the word an impossibility of bearing witness. And this and nothing else is its truth.

VI

In every age humankind has known another experience of language, in which the truth of an assertion does not depend on verification of the correspondence between words and things. This is the oath, that is, the linguistic act that performatively produces as a fact the *dictum* to which it is added. From this perspective, the distinction between promissory oath, which cannot be false, and assertoric oath, which can be true or false, corresponds to a phase in which the oath had lost its original performative force. As is shown by the archaic trial, which in both Greece and Rome took the form of a contraposition between two oaths, the original issue was not the evidence for the truth of an assertion but the greater or lesser force of the oath, its greater or lesser conformity with the ritual formula that defined *ius*. The judge did not decide which oath was true or false but declared which should be considered the *sacramentum iustum* and which the *sacramentum iniustum*. In place of the veritative relation between language and the world the oath substitutes a stronger nexus that guarantees, so to speak, magically—that is, juridically—the equivalence between words and things.

In testimony there is nothing that can guarantee such a nexus. The truth at issue in testimony, even if expressed in words, does not consist in the correspondence between things and what is said. Unlike in the oath, in testimony what is at issue is not the force of the word, but its weakness. The witness bears witness to the constitutive inability of language to state the truth in an assertoric way. And yet, the witness does not have recourse to another place for the truth, another possible way into it that is not language. The witness believes in words, despite their fragility, and remains to the last a philologist, lover of the word. But of the word not as an assertion: as a gesture

This is why Plato defines Alcestis's gesture of offering to die for Admetus as 'testimony' (*marturia*, Symposium 179b6). Testimony of what? Of love, certainly ('Because of her love,' Plato writes, 'she went so far beyond [Admetus's] parents in family feeling [*philia*]').[6] But not

---

6 Plato, *Symposium* (Alexander Nehamas and Paul Woodruff trans.) in *Complete Works* (John M. Cooper ed.) (Indianapolis, IN: Hackett, 1997), p. 464.

just this. As in Rilke's poem, Alcestis must have spoken to the god ('She is speaking to the god, and the god listens, / and all can hear, as though within the god.'), but the testimony is not constituted by her words.[7] And yet no one can doubt what she has said to the god; no one raises the question of its truth. Alcestis is a witness because in her words she has put her very life at stake.

The witness renounces the verifiability of her words, but not because she has available, like the oath taker, a stronger nexus, a *horkos*, a sacred object that she clutches in her hands as she speaks. At the point of giving testimony, the witness is abandoned by every guarantee and every external resource; she is absolutely alone. Just as Alcestis is suddenly alone amid the people who surround her. Her gestures, her words are similar to those we speak and whisper when no one sees us. This is why the witness

7 Rainer Maria Rilke, 'Alcestis' in *The Selected Poetry of Rainer Maria Rilke* (Stephen Mitchell ed. and trans.) (New York: Random House, 1982), p. 57.

cannot lie; she no longer has any need to deceive—not even herself. Testimony is constitutively in abandon; no one can bear witness for the witness, not even the witness.

VII

This can also be expressed by saying that the witness is alone with his words, that that for which—in every sense of the preposition 'for'—he bears witness is first and foremost language. But what does it mean to bear witness for language? What need does language have for testimonies? Certainly, every language needs a speaker and contains within itself the site on which the speaker locates himself in order to take up the word, in order to say 'I.' 'I' is the place in which the living being and language for a moment coincide—that is, fall together—in a voice. But to say 'I', to assume the position of a speaker in a language, is not yet to bear witness.

In order to be able to speak, in order to say 'I,' the subject must, so to speak, forget language, forget that he is speaking and immerge himself unreservedly in the river of meaningful propositions, of opinions endowed with sense. He can also, if he wants, speak nonsense. But in each case, he is not alone with his language and cannot bear witness to it. Testimony is the experience of language that remains when all sentences have been said, all opinions endowed with sense have been offered—or at least are supposed to have been. When, that is, the speaker realizes that he is truly alone with his language—not with the countless propositions within the language but with language itself, which is silent. When he understands for the first time that he is speaking, that he has irrevocably, poetically put his life in question in language, that he can no longer speak in order to communicate something to someone.

In this sense the poet is a witness par excellence. Indeed, the language of poetry is the language that remains when all the communicative and informative functions have been deactivated, when the poet cannot turn to anyone else—not even himself—but solely to language. The poet find himself marvellously and irreparably alone with his word, and can bear witness to that word.

Reflection—the 'I think'—is instead the point where the speaker who is about to discover himself unwillingly to be witness and poet finds a mirror in which to escape solitude, a last refuge from which he can still somehow offer meaningful discourse and propositions. We all cling to the 'I' in order to escape from the solitary encounter with language, in order not to be constrained to poetry. This is the meaning of Hölderlin's stubborn critique of reflection, the experience that separates him from his companions Schelling and Hegel.

Whoever has had this profound (in fact, bottomless) experience, whoever finds himself immedicably alone with the silence of his language, can be—as has happened—

accused of madness, and can also even accept that others believe him to be so. This is Hölderlin's choice when he withdraws to the tower on the Neckar, when he says he is no longer named Hölderlin but rather Scardanelli or Buonarroti or Rosetti—names of a writer whose poems others find lacking all logical connection, hymns in which parataxis and the isolation of words eliminate all discourse from the language and make it appear finally as such, in its poverty and its glory. Poetry is the language in which one bears witness for language.

VIII

What does it mean to bear witness for language? The language at issue in testimony seems to be a language that says nothing, a language that has nothing to say. But this is exactly where testimony is decided, where it is separated from every other experience of language. Indeed, nothingness is the final limit a philosophy reaches if it does not pass over into testimony. Nothing is the experience that

there is language but that there is no world. Nothing is
the name of a language left with no world. As Leonardo
intuited when he wrote 'what is called nothingness is
found only in time and words', this means that the experience of nothingness is still an experience of language,
that this experience does not call into question language's
primacy. It marks the threshold beyond which alone testimony can begin. Whoever dwells on this threshold,
whoever holds fast on to the place of nothingness, cannot
bear witness for language.

One can express the experience at issue in testimony by
saying that what the witness experiences is, to the exact
contrary, that there is no language, that it is possible not
to have a language. But what defines his testimony is that
through this absence of language he bears witness for language, brings to words a lack of words. The witness stubbornly stands in place of language, there where words are
lacking—he is the placeholder of language. Just as the gestures of deaf-mutes signify words that they cannot utter,

so the sublime miming of testimony shows language for the first time.

IX

Bearing witness for language concerns names, not propositions. Just as terms are torn from their semantic context and restored to their status as pure names in the late hymns of Hölderlin, so in the language of testimony sentences are reduced to a succession of caesuras and staccati, similar to a field of ruins upon which single lemmas and words stick out—even simple particles, as in Hölderlin the adversative conjunction *aber*, 'but'.

Testimony is an idiom made up solely of vocatives, that is, words that do not signify other people and things but rather call them by name. It is an impossible task because the vocative is an interruption of the statement in which it appears and has no syntactic relation to the rest of the proposition. One cannot offer a meaningful discourse made solely of breakages, a continuum of interruptions.

When speaking the witness does not say but, rather, calls—insistently continues to call—and it is the tenacity of this meaningless apostrophe that constitutes his sole, inescapable authority.

X

The relation between testimony and philosophy is the subject of a brief, brilliant text by Gianni Carchia, in which he interrogates the difference between testimony and method. Indeed, the reduction of testimony to method is 'the tenacious temptation of the *logos* of philosophy.' What method seeks to eliminate from testimony is its irremediable factuality, its being an event and not the result of any argumentation. 'To bear witness means, first of all, to affirm the character of truth as an occurrence . . . the absolute asymmetry of the truth with respect to the intentional consciousness.' Testimony, one could say, begins exactly when every predetermined way to the truth—every *methodos*—vanishes. It is because he finds himself suddenly without a way to the truth that the witness can only bear witness to it. Hence the inadequacy, according to Carchia, of both the Husserlian opposition between horizon consciousness and object consciousness and the Heideggerian passage from an ontic dimension to an ontological opening. In both there remains something like a 'primacy of intentionality', and the break with method is not truly achieved. 'Only the encounter with the most radical alterity merits the name of testimony' and this encounter entails the suspension of all community to such a degree that 'incommunicability and solipsism are the deep, essential mark of bearing witness'.

It is not surprising that at this point Carchia opposes the transcendence of testimony to the immanence of method. 'The passage from the immanence of method to the transcendence of testimony presupposes something like a conversion, a *metabasis eis allo genos*.' A correction of terminology is, however, necessary here. Testimony is defined by neither transcendence nor immanence. Rather, it lies in their coincidence, like the 'immanent cause' that Spinoza exemplifies with the meaning of a peculiar verbal form in the Hebrew language that expresses an action in which the agent and patient, active and passive, become one. Here a cause, by definition transcendent to its effects, acts on itself and becomes in some way immanent.

That is to say, testimony has to do with a capacity to be affected, at the point where it is not affected by an external object—or not only by it—but also, and above all, by its own receptivity. The speaking being who is affected not by what it says but by its capacity to speak and to remain silent can bear witness. Just as a subject that is not affected by an object but by its own affectability does not know something but, rather, only a knowability, so too the witness feels within himself the birth not of the sound of a saying—but, rather, the silence of a sayability. The purely sayable language that is produced in this experience that is at once active and passive, transcendent and immanent, is the language of testimony, the language for which and in place of which the witness bears witness. It is a word that does not say something about something, but the pure existence, at once and in the same gesture, of the name and of the thing named: testimony, that is, of the truth and nothing but the truth.

In this sense we can say that to bear witness means to hold oneself in relation not to a knowledge but to a zone of non-knowledge, that whoever bears witness can be ignorant of that to which he is bearing witness, but, like Socrates, does not repress his not knowing, remains faithful to his unknowingness. The manners and the ways through which we do not know are, if we are aware of them, just as decisive as the ways in which we know.

This does not mean to introduce the fogginess of mysticism into thought, but, exactly the opposite, to grasp for the first time what is at stake in the experience that we define with that name, which in truth is nothing vague at all. When the last scholarch of the Platonic academy in exile in Persia tried to express the supreme principle of thought in words, he felt the need to state clearly that when we say that it is unknowable or unsayable our discourse is reversed and no longer refers to an object but to ourselves and to our faculty of knowing. This is the arduous reversal that the witness experiences. In the zone of non-knowledge that opens up for him here there are neither 'night' nor 'clouds' but only the limpid and perfectly intelligible experience of a pure potentiality for knowing and saying, with nothing to say or to know. Precisely the experience of a pure language, a pure word. And this word, which says nothing if not an impossibility of saying, the witness cannot hold back because, once again, no one bears witness for the witness.

XI

Truth is an errancy, without which a certain person could not live. That is to say, it is a form of life; it is the form of life which that certain person cannot do without. His form-of-life is, in this sense, an errancy for the truth that constitutes him as witness.

If man is in errancy for the truth, he is to the same degree in errancy for non-truth. He can, that is, not bear witness but tell lies. How long can someone lie before ceasing to be human? There is, in truth, no limit. The human being is one who can wander errantly without limit within and for untruth and within and for the truth. This is exactly what constitutes humankind's errancy as a history that can, eventually, come to an end but is in itself without end.

The witness who cannot enunciate the truth can denounce falsehood. The denunciation of untruth is not, however, a testimony. It is a prophecy that, as such, cannot be heard by those who have lost the truth. And yet, when asked 'if this is a man' we must answer: yes, one who lies is still a man who, insofar as he wanders for untruth, still has in some way to do with the truth. Only if lies could remain silent, only if there could be a silent lie, then every errancy for the truth would cease, and, with this, the possibility of bearing witness.

The search for a post-history, for an ulterior time without historical errancy is inherent in falsehood, and just as much in vain. The witness instead knows that his testimony interrupts history and the discourse of lies, without inaugurating an ulterior time and discourse, and knows that there is no history of truth, only a history of falsehood.